Our Global Community

Markets

Cassie Mayer

Heinemann Library

Customer Service 888-454-2279
Visit our website at www.heinemannraintree.com

Designed by Joanna Hinton-Malivoire
Photo research by Ruth Smith
Printed and bound in China by South China Printing Co. Ltd.

11 10 09 08 07
10 9 8 7 6 5 4 3 2 1

The Library of Congress has cataloged the first edition of this book as follows:
Mayer, Cassie.
  Markets / Cassie Mayer.
     p. cm. -- (Our global community)
  Includes bibliographical references and index.
  ISBN-13: 978-1-4034-9404-7 (hc)
  ISBN-13: 978-1-4034-9413-9 (pb)
  1. Markets--Juvenile literature. I. Title.
  HF5470.M397 2007
  381'.1--dc22
                          2006034296

Acknowledgements
The publishers would like to thank the following for permission to reproduce photographs: Alamy Images pp. **11** (Charles Bowman), **12** (David R. Frazier Photolibrary, Inc), **16** (Greenshoots Communications), **18** (Glen Allison), **23** (Charles Bowman); Corbis pp. **4** (Michael S. Lewis), **6** (Frans Lemmens/zefa), **7** (Barry Lewis), **8** (Bob Rowan; Progressive Image), **9** (Kevin Fleming), **10** (Jon Hicks), **13** (Michael Prince), **14** (Owen Franken), **15** (Hubert Stadler), **17** (Owen Franken), **19** (Dung Vo Trung), **20** (Tibor Bognár), **21** (Bob Krist), **22** (Barry Lewis), **23** (Michael S. Lewis; Barry Lewis); Getty Images pp. **5** (Stone).

Cover photograph reproduced with permission of Corbis/Tibor Bognar. Back cover photograph reproduced with permission of Getty Images/Stone.

Every effort has been made to contact copyright holders of any material reproduced in this book. Any omissions will be rectified in subsequent printings if notice is given to the publishers.

The paper used to print this books comes from sustainable resources.

Contents

Markets Around the World

People shop at markets.

Markets sell many things.

spices

People sell things at markets.

vendor

People buy things with money.

Types of Markets

Markets are big.

Markets are small.

Markets are on streets.

Markets are in malls.

What Markets Sell

Markets sell fish.

Markets sell meat.

Markets sell bread.

Markets sell cheese.

Markets sell clothes.

Markets sell toys.

Special Markets

Markets are on water.

Markets are open at night.

Markets are special wherever you go.

People need markets.

Market Vocabulary

vendor

buyer

Picture Glossary

 **mall** a big building that has shops and markets in it

 **market** a place where you can buy things

 **vendor** a person who sells things. Vendors work at markets.

Index

Note to Parents and Teachers
This series expands children's horizons beyond their neighborhoods to show that communities around the world share similar features and rituals of daily life. The text has been chosen with the advice of a literacy expert to ensure that beginners can read the books independently or with moderate support. Stunning photographs visually support the text while engaging students with the material.

You can support children's nonfiction literacy skills by helping students use the table of contents, headings, picture glossary, and index.